SPACE FLIGHT ADVENTURES AND D

TRAILBLAZING ASTRONAUT JOHN GLENN

A MYREPORTLINKS.COM BOOK

HENRY M. HOLDEN

MyReportLinks.com Books

an imprint of

Enslow Publishers, Inc.

Box 398, 40 Industrial Road
Berkeley Heights, NJ 07922
USA

MyReportLinks.com Books, an imprint of Enslow Publishers, Inc. MyReportLinks®
is a registered trademark of Enslow Publishers, Inc.

Library of Congress Cataloging-in-Publication Data

Holden, Henry M.
  Trailblazing astronaut John Glenn / Henry M. Holden.
      p. cm. — (Space flight adventures and disasters)
Summary: A biography of former Senator John Glenn, who orbited the earth
in 1962 and became the oldest man to go into space in 1998.
Includes bibliographical references and index.
  ISBN 0-7660-5166-8
  1. Glenn, John, 1921—-Juvenile literature. 2. Astronauts—United
States—Biography—Juvenile literature. 3. Legislators—United
States—Biography—Juvenile literature. [1. Glenn, John, 1921– 2.
Astronauts. 3. Legislators.] I. Title. II. Series.
  TL789.85.G6H65 2004
  629.45'0092—dc22

                                      2003014487

Printed in the United States of America

10 9 8 7 6 5 4 3 2 1

To Our Readers:
Through the purchase of this book, you and your library gain access to the Report Links that specifically back up this book.
The Publisher will provide access to the Report Links that back up this book and will keep these Report Links up to date on **www.myreportlinks.com** for three years from the book's first publication date.
We have done our best to make sure all Internet addresses in this book were active and appropriate when we went to press. However, the author and the Publisher have no control over, and assume no liability for, the material available on those Internet sites or on other Web sites they may link to.
The usage of the MyReportLinks.com Books Web site is subject to the terms and conditions stated on the Usage Policy Statement on **www.myreportlinks.com**.
A password may be required to access the Report Links that back up this book. The password is found on the bottom of page 4 of this book.
Any comments or suggestions can be sent by e-mail to comments@myreportlinks.com or to the address on the back cover.

Contents

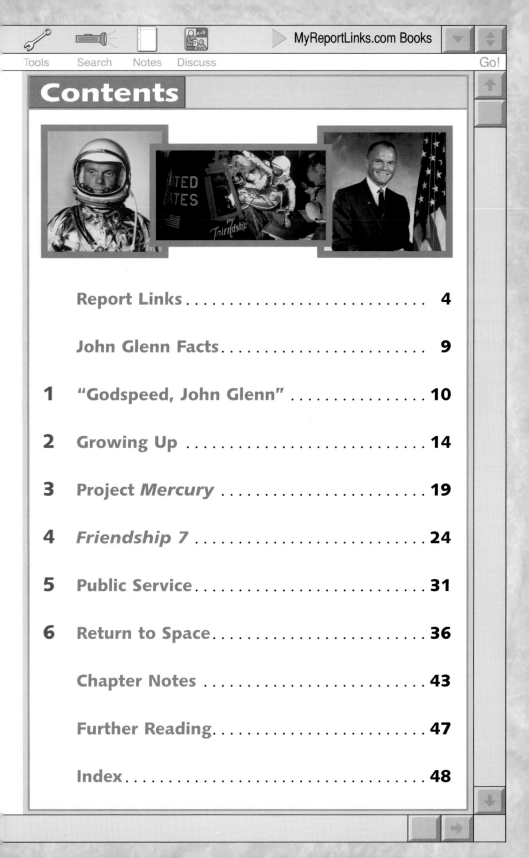

MyReportLinks.com Books
Great Books, Great Links, Great for Research!

The Report Links listed on the following four pages can save you hours of research time by **instantly** bringing you to the best Web sites relating to your report topic.

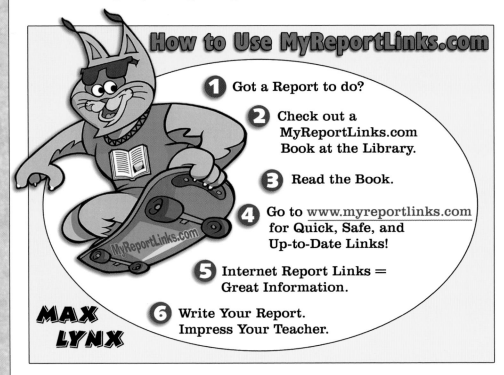

How to Use MyReportLinks.com

1 Got a Report to do?

2 Check out a MyReportLinks.com Book at the Library.

3 Read the Book.

4 Go to www.myreportlinks.com for Quick, Safe, and Up-to-Date Links!

5 Internet Report Links = Great Information.

6 Write Your Report. Impress Your Teacher.

MAX LYNX

The pre-evaluated Web sites are your links to source documents, photographs, illustrations, and maps. They also provide links to dozens—even hundreds—of Web sites about your report subject.

MyReportLinks.com Books and the MyReportLinks.com Web site save you time and make report writing easier than ever!

Please see "To Our Readers" on the copyright page for important information about this book, the MyReportLinks.com Web site, and the Report Links that back up this book. Please enter **FJG8930** if asked for a password.

The Internet sites described below can be accessed at
http://www.myreportlinks.com

*EDITOR'S CHOICE

▶**John Glenn: The Right Stuff**
At this PBS Web site you can read a brief profile of John Glenn. You
will learn about his accomplishments as an astronaut, a World War II
and Korean War veteran, and a United States Senator.

*EDITOR'S CHOICE

▶**Biographical Data: John Glenn**
At the Lyndon B. Johnson Space Center you will find a brief profile of
John Glenn. Here you will learn about his life, experience with NASA,
special honors he has received, and his space flight experience.

*EDITOR'S CHOICE

▶**John Glenn**
This Kodak Web site contains a photographic history of John Glenn.
Here you will find a brief profile of his life and learn about
the *Mercury 6* and *Discovery* missions. You will also find images of space.

*EDITOR'S CHOICE

▶**The 40th Anniversary of the *Mercury Seven***
At the 40th Anniversary of the *Mercury Seven* Web site you can read the
profile of all crew members, including John Glenn. You will also find a
time line of events, photo gallery, and documents related to the mission.

*EDITOR'S CHOICE

▶**John Glenn: Return to Space**
The CNN Web site follows the story of John Glenn and his 1998
return to space on the *Discovery* space shuttle. Click on "Photo Gallery"
to view images of John Glenn on his 1962 and 1998 missions.

*EDITOR'S CHOICE

▶**Glenn, *Discovery* Crew Visit NIH, Recount
Historic Space Journey**
The National Institute of Health Web site discusses John Glenn and the
Discovery crew's return from space.

Report Links

The Internet sites described below can be accessed at http://www.myreportlinks.com

▶ **Astronaut John Glenn and the *Friendship 7* Mission**

The National Archives & Records Administration holds the transcripts of communication from John Glenn's reentry on the *Friendship 7* mission.

▶ **Cold War Experience: Technology**

Explore the history of the Cold War and the space race. View an interactive time line beginning with the launch of *Sputnik* in 1957, and learn about American and Soviet scientists.

▶ **"A Giant Leap for Mankind"**

From *Life* magazine comes this overview of space history. Topics covered include the Cold War, how the space race began, rocket science, *Mercury 7*, and moon landings.

▶ **Glenn, John Herschel, Jr., 1921–**

John Glenn was an Ohio state senator from 1974 until 1999. The Biographical Directory of the United States Senate Web site details his life and accomplishments.

▶ **Glenn Research Center**

At the Glenn Research Web site you can learn about aeronautics, aerospace, flight systems, and John Glenn's contributions to NASA projects.

▶ **John Glenn: Return to Space**

The *National Geographic* Web site documents John Glenn's return to space through seven previously unpublished photographs.

▶ **John Glenn—Space Pioneer**

Find out about John Glenn and his missions in space at this site.

▶ **John Glenn: Still the Right Stuff**

An essay about John Glenn's return to space can be found on this Web page. There are also many images of the crew as they prepare for their mission.

Tools   Search   Notes   Discuss

MyReportLinks.com Books

Go!

Report Links

The Internet sites described below can be accessed at
http://www.myreportlinks.com

▶**John Glenn Archives**

The John Glenn Archives Web site lets you explore John Glenn's Senate papers, the *Friendship 7* mission, and a chronology of events in Glenn's life.

▶**John Glenn *Friendship 7* Spacesuit**

At this Smithsonian Web site you can view an image of John Glenn's space suit.

▶**Kennedy Space Center**

The Kennedy Space Center's Web site has articles about the center's history, space shuttles, and the latest news from "NASA Direct."

▶**Major John H. Glenn, Jr., Exchange Pilot**

A brief profile of John Glenn's military career. He served in World War II and the Korean War.

▶**Milestones of Flight**

Discover monumental events in flight history, including *Mercury Friendship 7*.

▶**NASA History Office**

The NASA History Office allows you to explore the history of NASA. You will learn about its official start in 1958 and its major accomplishments since.

▶**NASA Human Space Flight**

At the NASA Human Space Flight Web site you can explore space stations and space shuttles. Learn about missions, and find out what happens behind the scenes. You can also get the latest "Space News."

▶**NASA Kids**

You can explore "Rockets and Airplanes," "Earth," "Astronauts Living in Space," "Space and Beyond," and many other interesting topics at the NASA Kids Web site.

The Internet sites described below can be accessed at
http://www.myreportlinks.com

▶**Online Shuttle Press Kit**

Learn about space shuttle missions, including STS-95, at the Online Shuttle Press Kit
Web site. The International Space Station, and Soviet missions, are discussed as well.

▶*Red Files*

PBS's *Red Files* studies the relationship between the United States and the Soviet
Union in the race to the moon. It includes brief biographies of key players, maps,
and interviews.

▶**The Right Stuff: Pioneer John Glenn Returns to Space**

FactMonster.com provides a profile of John Glenn and his accomplishments. You
will also find links to information about NASA, the *Apollo 11* moonwalk, and other
related sites.

▶**Rocket Man**

PBS's Online *News Hour with Jim Lehrer* holds the transcript to an interview with
NASA administrator Daniel Goldin. They talk about Senator John Glenn's return to
space on the *Discovery* space shuttle.

▶**Russia Remembers Space Hero**

At this BBC News Web site you can read a brief profile of cosmonaut Yuri Gagarin,
the first man in space. Links to other articles about Gagarin and his accomplishments
are included.

▶**Space Race**

Explore the origins of the space race, the Soviet Union's space history, and learn about
satellites at the Space Race Web site.

▶**Special Message to the Congress on Urgent National Needs**

At this Web site you can read a speech by John F. Kennedy where he discusses the
need for America to be the first to land on the moon.

▶**Today In History**

Today In History, a Library of Congress Web site, tells the story of the day John
F. Kennedy requested that Lyndon B. Johnson put together a satellite program.

John Glenn Facts

1921—*July 18:* Born in Cambridge, Ohio.

1939—Enrolls in Muskingum College.

1942—Leaves school to become a U.S. Marine Corps pilot.

1943—*April 1:* Marries Anna "Annie" Castor.

1943–1945—Serves as a pilot in World War II.

1948–1950—Works as a flight instructor of advanced flight training in the U.S. Marine Corps.

1950–1953—Serves as a pilot in the Korean War.

1953—Becomes a test pilot for the U.S. Navy.

1957—*July 16:* Sets a transcontinental speed record in Project Bullet, flying from Los Angeles to New York City in three hours and twenty-three minutes.

1959—NASA chooses Glenn for the *Mercury* program.

1962—*Feb. 20:* Becomes the first American to orbit the earth, on *Friendship 7.*

—Receives a Bachelor of Science degree in chemistry from Muskingum College.

1964—*Jan.:* Resigns from NASA.

—Withdraws from the Ohio primary as a democratic candidate for the U.S. Senate.

—Becomes a colonel in the U.S. Marines Corps.

1965—Retires from the Marines.

—Becomes an executive for Royal Crown International.

—Becomes a consultant for NASA.

1970—Loses the Ohio Democratic primary for U.S. Senate.

1974—Elected U.S. senator from Ohio.

1978—Helps write the Nuclear Non-Proliferation Act.

1980—Reelected U.S. senator from Ohio.

1986—Reelected U.S. senator from Ohio.

1992—Reelected U.S. senator from Ohio. Becomes the first Ohio senator to be elected four consecutive times.

1998—*Jan.:* NASA chooses Glenn to return to space aboard the space shuttle *Discovery.*

—*Oct. 29–Nov. 7:* Becomes the oldest person to fly in space.

"GODSPEED, JOHN GLENN"

It was February 20, 1962. John Glenn, dressed in a silver space suit, sat inside the cramped *Friendship 7* capsule. The odd-looking, bell-shaped craft would soon carry him into space, on top of a rocket. This tiny craft was not much larger than a phone booth.

▲ Astronaut John Glenn enters into Friendship 7 *before making history as the first American to orbit the earth. He once joked that one did not "climb into the* Mercury *spacecraft. You put it on."*

The launch had been put off eight times because of bad weather and mechanical issues.[1] The delays, while annoying, were helpful. "I continued to study and work out in the simulation trainers," said Glenn. "I practiced particularly hard at hand-controlling the capsule."[2]

Launch

At 9:47 A.M. Eastern time, the Atlas V rocket, carrying *Friendship 7*, rose off the launch pad at Cape Canaveral, Florida. "Godspeed, John Glenn," said astronaut Scott Carpenter, in Mission Control.[3] The 168-pound (76.2-kilogram) John Glenn was riding a rocket that had 3.5 million horsepower.[4]

About two minutes after launch, the two booster engines shut down and dropped away. Glenn was traveling 25,750 feet per second (7,848 meters per second), four miles (6.4 kilometers) for every heartbeat in his chest. He was weightless, over one hundred miles (160.9 kilometers) above the earth. Astronaut Alan Shepard called and said, "You have a 'Go' for at least seven orbits."[5]

A Major Problem

Glenn did not know it at the time, but he had a problem. Engineers on the ground noticed a light indicating the spacecraft's heat shield was not locked in position. Glenn did not have this light on his panel. The heat shield protects the capsule and astronaut during the fiery reentry. If the shield failed, Glenn would become a fireball. The signal could be an error, but there was no way to tell. Instead of seven orbits, Mission Control would bring Glenn down after only three orbits.

The retropack has rockets that slow the spacecraft down during reentry. Mission Control decided that after slowing the craft down, the retropack, which attaches to the heat shield, would not be released. They were hoping the pack would keep the shield in place during reentry. This should work if all the rockets in the retropack fired. If they did not, the retropack would have to be released. Any unburned rocket fuel would then ignite during reentry and safely burn up in Earth's atmosphere.

▲ *Glenn smiles aboard the USS* Noa. *He and the* Friendship 7 *capsule were collected by crane from the Atlantic Ocean twenty-one minutes after falling into the water.*

The retropack would burn away at this time, but they hoped that by this point the pressures would be strong enough to keep the shield in place.

More than four hours after launch, the retropack fired. About six minutes later, Glenn pitched the spacecraft up to the correct attitude for its plunge back to Earth.[6]

Now came the critical moment. As the air heated around the capsule, it became electrically charged. This blocked all radio communications between Glenn and Mission Control. For about seven minutes, Mission Control listened to the empty crackle in their headphones.[7] Then, the voice of John Glenn came over the radio, "Boy, that was a real fireball."[8] He was safely dangling from the huge parachute holding the capsule.

At 2:43 P.M. Eastern time, *Friendship 7* splashed down southeast of Bermuda. Glenn had traveled 81,000 miles (130,357 kilometers) in four hours and fifty-six minutes. The destroyer USS *Noa* spotted the main parachute and had the spacecraft aboard twenty-one minutes later. Glenn returned to a hero's welcome. He became the most honored American explorer since aviator Charles Lindbergh.[9]

GROWING UP

John Herschel Glenn, Jr., was born to Clara and John Herschel Glenn, Sr., on July 18, 1921. Glenn has one younger adopted sister, Jean. The Glenn family lived in Cambridge, Ohio, before moving to New Concord, Ohio, when he was two years old. Although named for his father, Glenn never used the name "Junior." Instead, his friends called him "Bud."[1]

John Glenn's boyhood was filled with the usual games: football, fishing, and making model airplanes.[2] The summer he turned eight, young John saw his first airplane, a WACO biplane. A biplane has two sets of wings and two seats, one behind the other. His father asked him, "You want to go up, Bud?" Glenn jumped at the chance. John was small enough to fit in the seat with his father. They flew over Cambridge a few times and then landed. "When I got out of the plane I was elated. I couldn't get the view from the air out of my mind, and the feeling of being suspended without falling. . . . I was hooked on flying after that, on the idea of swooping and soaring."[3]

John attended school in New Concord, Ohio. After graduating high school, he enrolled in Muskingum College, also in New Concord.

▶ World War II

Glenn had thought of becoming a doctor.[4] That changed on a Sunday morning in December 1941. The twenty-year-old Glenn was on his way to church to hear Anna

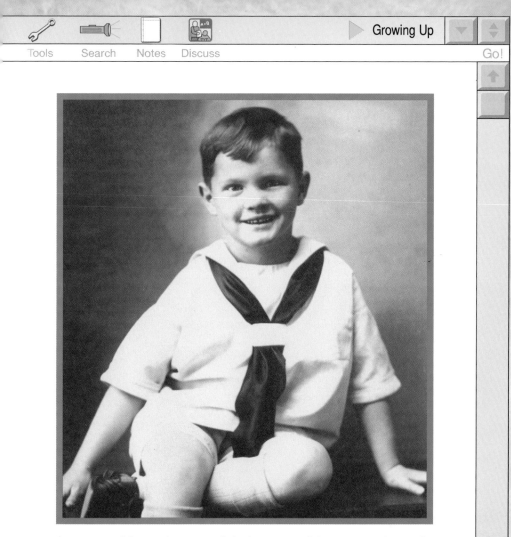

▲ As a small boy, John enjoyed climbing trees, fishing, pretending to be a pilot, and swimming.

"Annie" Castor give a music recital. Glenn had grown up and gone to school with Annie. She was his childhood sweetheart and now his fiancée. "She and I had planned to be married after we were out of college," said Glenn. That changed when he heard the news on the radio that the Japanese had bombed Pearl Harbor: ". . . [W]e sat and talked that evening, and decided my responsibility was to go."[5] Glenn dropped out of college in his junior year and joined the Army Air Corps.

△ *John Glenn when he was a naval air cadet at the age of twenty. In 1943, Glenn earned his aviator wings as a Marine after enlisting in the U.S. Naval Reserve a year earlier.*

Glenn took the Army physical examination, passed, and was sworn in. After several months went by without orders, Glenn took the Navy's physical. He passed and was sworn into the Naval Aviation Cadet Program in March 1942. Glenn already had his private pilots license through a government civilian pilot training program. This license allowed students to start learning how to fly while they were completing their education. Glenn's Navy orders came right away, and he left for training. He graduated with his gold pilot wings and a commission in the U.S. Marine Corps in 1943. Soon after, he married Annie Castor.

During his World War II service, Glenn flew fifty-nine combat missions. He stayed in the Marine Corps after the war. During the Korean War, he flew sixty-three missions.[6] As an exchange pilot with the Air Force, Glenn shot down three enemy planes in the closing days of the war. For his service in two wars, Glenn received many honors. These included the Distinguished Flying Cross six times, and the Air Medal with eighteen clusters.

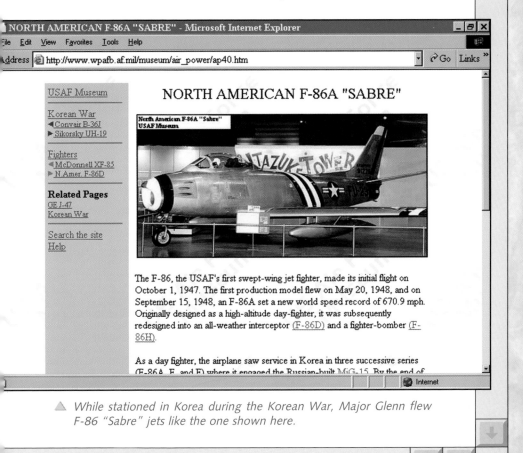

NORTH AMERICAN F-86A "SABRE" - Microsoft Internet Explorer

File   Edit   View   Favorites   Tools   Help

Address http://www.wpafb.af.mil/museum/air_power/ap40.htm   Go   Links

USAF Museum

Korean War
◄ Convair B-36J
► Sikorsky UH-19

Fighters
◄ McDonnell XF-85
► N.Amer. F-86D

Related Pages
GE J-47
Korean War

Search the site
Help

NORTH AMERICAN F-86A "SABRE"

The F-86, the USAF's first swept-wing jet fighter, made its initial flight on October 1, 1947. The first production model flew on May 20, 1948, and on September 15, 1948, an F-86A set a new world speed record of 670.9 mph. Originally designed as a high-altitude day-fighter, it was subsequently redesigned into an all-weather interceptor (F-86D) and a fighter-bomber (F-86H).

As a day fighter, the airplane saw service in Korea in three successive series (F-86A, E, and F) where it engaged the Russian-built MiG-15. By the end of

▲ While stationed in Korea during the Korean War, Major Glenn flew F-86 "Sabre" jets like the one shown here.

Test Pilot School

After the Korean War, John Glenn graduated from the U.S. Navy's Test Pilot School. A test pilot is a dangerous job. Glenn was test firing new cannons on an FJ–3 Fury jet. He was at forty-four thousand feet, when he heard a pop in the cockpit. The air began to rush in. At this altitude, the air is "thin" and there is not enough oxygen to breath. At the same moment, the oxygen regulator stopped. Glenn switched to the backup, but it also failed. Within a few seconds, Glenn knew he was in serious trouble. ". . . my eyesight started deteriorating rapidly. . . . I was eight miles high, with only a few seconds of vision left, and not many more of consciousness."[7] Glenn had a small backup bottle of oxygen in his parachute. He put the airplane into a steep dive and groped for the wooden ball at the end of a cable. This would activate the oxygen. "The black patches painted my vision down to near nothingness. My lungs were bursting. . . . I was on the verge of unconsciousness. . . ."[8] Glenn pulled on the ball, and oxygen flowed into his lungs. He pulled the airplane out of the dive and flew back to his base.

In 1957, Glenn found himself assigned to an office job. He really wanted to fly, so he convinced the Pentagon on the idea of a supersonic flight across the United States, to set a new speed record.[9] It was called Project Bullet. Glenn was flying again. He set a speed record by flying from Los Angeles to New York in three hours, twenty-three minutes. He was the first person ever to average supersonic speeds on a coast-to-coast flight. Supersonic speed is traveling faster than the speed of sound.

Glenn wanted to fly even faster and higher. Project *Mercury* would be the way to achieve this.

PROJECT MERCURY

On October 7, 1957, the Soviet Union launched *Sputnik I.* It was the first artificial satellite to orbit Earth. The small sphere, about the size of a basketball, contained scientific instruments. It weighed about 184 pounds (83.5 kilograms). A month later, the Soviet Union launched *Sputnik II.* It weighed more than a thousand pounds (453.6 kilograms), had instruments, and carried a dog.

▶ The Space Race

On January 31, 1958, America launched its first satellite, *Explorer I.* The satellite was in the shape of a pencil and weighed about thirty pounds (13.6 kilograms). In May, the Soviet Union launched a satellite that weighed nearly three thousand

The Soviet Union launched Sputnik II on November 3, 1957. It carried the first living creature to reach orbit, a dog named Laika. Laika died on the fourth day of the mission due to high temperatures inside of the capsule.

pounds (1,361 kilograms). America knew that rockets that could lift heavy, unmanned satellites could also send a human into space.[1] America thought the Soviet Union might try to use satellites as military weapons. The "space race" was on.

On December 17, 1958, the National Aeronautics and Space Administration (NASA) announced the first manned satellite program, Project *Mercury*. They planned six flights. The objectives of the program were to orbit a manned spacecraft around Earth, study the possibility of humans living in space, and recover both the man and spacecraft safely.

The *Mercury* capsule was barely large enough to hold one person. Inside were more than one hundred controls and fifty-five electrical switches.[2] Before any humans went into space, substitute passengers tested the space-craft. Monkeys and chimpanzees were chosen. Their genetic makeup is similar to humans. They can also be trained to perform some tasks similar to those humans perform. All the animals returned safely from their trips.

▶ Project Astronaut

The *Mercury* astronauts came from a pool of five hundred men in excellent physical condition. They could not be older than forty years or taller than five feet, eleven inches (180.3 centimeters). They had to be test pilots with engineering training and at least 1,500 hours of flight experience. The men would be selected based on endurance and psychiatric tests. They endured severe vibration, acceleration, heat, noise, and other tests. This was to see if they could handle spaceflight.

In January 1961, NASA announced the seven military men who would be the nation's first astronauts: Alan B. Shepard, Virgil "Gus" I. Grissom, John H. Glenn, Jr.,

Walter M. Schirra, Jr., Donald K. Slayton, M. Scott Carpenter, and L. Gordon Cooper.

This was a group of brave and sometimes-wild bunch of guys. Most of them drove fast sports cars. Gus Grissom, Gordon Cooper, and Alan Shepard had Corvettes. Wally Schirra had a Triumph. Glenn, on the other hand, had a beat-up old Peugeot.[3] After long days in simulators, some of the astronauts liked to party. Glenn, however, was different. He kept reminding the others that they were public figures. "Whether we deserve it or not, people look up to us. So, we have a terrific responsibility. . . . We've got to be above even the appearance of doing wrong," he said.[4]

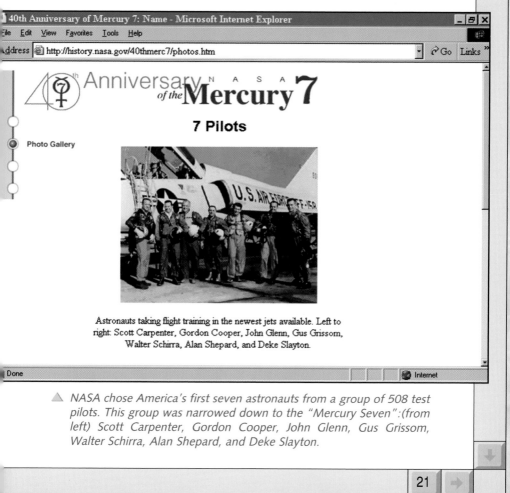

40th Anniversary of Mercury 7: Name - Microsoft Internet Explorer

File   Edit   View   Favorites   Tools   Help

Address http://history.nasa.gov/40thmerc7/photos.htm   Go   Links

Anniversary of the NASA **Mercury 7**

7 Pilots

Photo Gallery

Astronauts taking flight training in the newest jets available. Left to right: Scott Carpenter, Gordon Cooper, John Glenn, Gus Grissom, Walter Schirra, Alan Shepard, and Deke Slayton.

Done   Internet

▲ *NASA chose America's first seven astronauts from a group of 508 test pilots. This group was narrowed down to the "Mercury Seven":(from left) Scott Carpenter, Gordon Cooper, John Glenn, Gus Grissom, Walter Schirra, Alan Shepard, and Deke Slayton.*

Men in Space

In April 1961, the space race heated up. Soviet cosmonaut (the Russian term for astronaut) Yuri Gagarin lifted off in the capsule *Vostok I.* Gagarin made one complete orbit of the Earth. He was the first human to do so. In May, Alan Shepard made a suborbital spaceflight. A suborbital flight does not circle the earth. Shepard became the first

▲ *Alan Shepard was the first American in space.*

American in space. His total flight lasted about fifteen minutes. After Shepard's flight, President John F. Kennedy challenged America to land a man on the moon by the end of the decade. Project *Mercury* was America's first step toward that goal.

In July, Gus Grissom made a second suborbital flight. Glenn had served as backup pilot for Shepard and Grissom. After Grissom's flight, NASA began to prepare Glenn for a third suborbital flight. Then, in August, the Soviet Union launched cosmonaut Gherman Titov in *Vostok II*. Titov made 17.5 orbits of the earth. In November, Enos, a chimpanzee, went up on the *Mercury*-Atlas V space craft. He made two orbits.

Glenn and the other astronauts each had special jobs in the design of the *Mercury* spacecraft. Glenn's responsibility was cockpit layout and control functioning. The cockpit held the pilot in a specially shaped couch, surrounded by instruments. "The way this instrumentation is presented to the pilot—that is, where it appears, how close it is to him, how easy it is for him to see and quickly understand—is of vital importance," said Glenn.[5]

The United States Congress, which controls NASA's budget, was putting pressure on them to keep up with the Soviet Union. Pressure from the public was also building. NASA decided to end suborbital flights and go ahead with the first manned orbital flight. Glenn had helped design the *Mercury* capsule. Now it was his turn to ride it into space.

FRIENDSHIP 7

About two hours before liftoff, Glenn boarded the tiny spacecraft. He was seventy-four feet above the ground, and the rocket swayed in a heavy gust of wind. "If you moved back and forth in the couch, you could feel the entire vehicle moving very slightly," he said.[1]

The suspense was building. Ninety minutes before liftoff, while the crew was securing the hatch, a bolt broke. This caused a forty-minute delay. Another suspenseful moment came about six minutes before launch. The Bermuda tracking station had a power failure. It was a backup for Cape Canaveral. Without it working, there would be no launch. Glenn was relieved when the power was restored.[2]

Humans in Space

One purpose of Glenn's flight was to answer a question facing NASA. How do humans react to microgravity? Gravity is what holds us on the ground. Anytime we drop or throw something, we are watching gravity in action. Occurring in space, microgravity is a very weak effect of what is felt on Earth. If everything worked properly, Glenn would record his reactions to experiments in microgravity. One of the experiments Glenn performed was to read an eye chart. Researchers expected his eyes to swell and his vision to blur. "I was supposed to look at that (chart), and if the letters got blurry, I was to do an emergency reentry," he said. "We all laugh at that now, but it was a real concern."[3]

▷ The Launch

The Redstone rocket lifted the first two manned *Mercury* capsules. The Atlas V rocket, a modified ballistic missile that lifted Glenn's *Friendship 7*, was more powerful, but it was also dangerous. They tended to explode. Glenn was sitting on top of 350,000 pounds (158,757 kilograms) of liquid oxygen. "I went up on the roof to watch (an Atlas launch) and it got up about 200 feet (60.9 meters) and it blew," astronaut Wally Schirra said. "That got my attention."[4]

▲ Mercury 6 *launched at 9:47:39* A.M. *on February 20, 1962.*

The launch itself was one of four important steps to get Glenn into space safely. Each step required perfect timing. The second was at a point called "maximum q." This is where there is the highest aerodynamic force on the capsule. This came at about forty-five seconds after launch, at about thirty-five thousand feet (10,668 meters). There had been difficulties at this point in earlier *Mercury* flights. On an unmanned flight, the Atlas rocket blew up.[5] Glenn was asked whether he was afraid before the mission. "Humans always have fear of unknown situations, this is normal," he said. "The important thing is what we do about it. . . . The best antidote to fear is to know all we can about a situation."[6]

▷ Trouble in Orbit

During orbit, a computer controls the capsule's flight path by squirting out jets of hydrogen peroxide. Glenn first noticed trouble when the automatic control system allowed the spacecraft to drift. Glenn had practiced hand flying in the simulator, so he was ready for this. He switched to his manual control and put *Friendship 7* back in its proper orbit. "This . . . provided me with an opportunity to demonstrate what a man can do in controlling a spacecraft," he said. However, this limited the time he could spend on some of the experiments he wanted to carry out on the flight.[7]

A warning light indicated the fuel supply for the automatic system was down to 62 percent. Glenn would have to make sure the capsule did not drift off course. *Friendship 7* had three separate systems to prevent such a loss of control. A fully automatic system used sensor devices and a computer. This system was causing the trouble. It was not releasing the hydrogen peroxide properly.[8]

This made him use more fuel than the automatic system would have used if the system were working properly. If he used too much fuel, disaster faced Glenn on reentry. The capsule would not be able to tilt into proper position for the return to Earth.

Over the Indian Ocean on his first orbit, Glenn became the first American to witness the sunset from above one hundred miles (160.9 kilometers). "That was about the shortest day I've ever run into," he said.[9]

Fireflies in Space

Over Canton Island, he saw thousands of little "bright yellowish-green particles." They were swarming all around his capsule at each of the three sunrises he saw from

▲ *Alan Shepard (right) was the capsule communicator for John Glenn's Mercury 6 flight. Shepard had been the first American in space.*

space.[10] Glenn first thought the spacecraft was tumbling or that he was looking into a field of stars. When he looked out the capsule window, he realized he was still in a normal altitude. The "fireflies," as he called the specks, were streaming past his spacecraft from ahead. As *Friendship 7* flew over the Pacific into brighter sunlight, the "fireflies" disappeared. These were later thought to be particles of paint from the spacecraft.[11]

▶ Reentry

Following retrofire, Mission Control told Glenn to leave the retropack attached. "This decision required me to perform manually a number of operations which are normally automatically programmed during reentry," said Glenn.[12]

As Glenn's capsule fell through the atmosphere, he could see pieces of something breaking off and flying past the spacecraft. "I thought these flaming pieces might be parts of the heat shield breaking off," Glenn said.[13] A fearsome orange glow began to surround the capsule.

The Earth's atmosphere would slow the capsule down from 17,500 miles per hour (28,163.5 kilometers per hour) to about 1,300 miles per hour (2,092.2 kilometers per hour) in about three minutes. Gravity would return during reentry. Glenn would feel eight times his normal weight.[14] Then, the spacecraft began twisting so violently that Glenn could not control the ship. He wondered whether his capsule would remain stable down to an altitude where the drogue parachute could open safely. The drogue is the small chute that pulls the larger chute open.

About a minute before the parachute opened, the capsule's fuel supply ran out. Glenn could not control the twisting. At about 35,000 feet (10,668 meters), Glenn decided to deploy the drogue chute manually. If he did not, the spacecraft might flip upside down. Just as he lifted his hand toward the switch, the drogue opened. Suddenly the spacecraft straightened out, and the main chute blossomed. Mission Control reminded Glenn to deploy the landing bag. He flipped the switch; a green light confirmed the landing bag was in place. Then came a "clunk" as the impact bag dropped into position four feet below the capsule. Later, scientists would discover that the heat shield had been properly in place all along. The capsule was so hot, it sent up a cloud of steam when it hit the water.

▲ On February 23, 1962, President John F. Kennedy awarded Glenn with the NASA Distinguished Service Award Medal at Cape Canaveral, Florida.

Scientists learned much from this first orbital flight. They learned that even under stress and microgravity humans could act in situations where machines or monkeys did not perform well.

President John F. Kennedy flew to Cape Canaveral to meet Glenn and present him with the NASA Distinguished Service Medal. America had a new hero. Millions turned out in New York City for Glenn's ticker-tape parade.

▷ America Goes to the Moon

Glenn had achieved Project *Mercury*'s goals. Humans could survive in space, and they could be returned safely to Earth. The flight marked a major milestone in the space race.[15] It led to more orbital flights and in time, flights to the moon. It also led to the creation of the space shuttle program.

America was on its way to the moon, and Glenn wanted to be a part of it. After his flight, NASA gave him administrative work instead of more training for a moon flight. "Space travel is at the frontier of my profession. It is going to be accomplished and I want to be in on it," he said.[16] Because of his age, forty-two, it was unlikely that he would be part of a future lunar landing. Glenn was an important hero. President Kennedy may have made it known to NASA that he did not want Glenn to fly again and possibly risk losing him.[17]

As the months stretched into years, Glenn realized that they would not send him up into space again. John Glenn would not wait around forever. He was still young, and he wanted to serve his country. Glenn resigned from NASA in January 1964. The next day he announced plans to run for the Democratic nomination for a U.S. Senate seat from Ohio.

PUBLIC SERVICE

When asked why he entered politics, John Glenn said, "I look upon my entire life as service to my country," and "I've looked at most of my life as public service."[1] Growing up in a small town, Glenn never imagined he could one day become a United States senator.

▶ A Short Campaign

Glenn's first Senate campaign lasted about a month. One morning, Glenn slipped and hit his head on the bathtub. The injury produced swelling and bleeding in his inner ear. This affected his balance. Glenn suffered from dizziness, nausea, and ringing in his ears. He could not get out of bed for weeks. "Any but the slowest of head movements would make the whole world spin," he said.[2] He was suffering from an illness called traumatic vertigo. Weeks went by, and his recovery was slow. Doctors said he could not actively campaign. They said his injury would heal in eight to twelve months. Not wanting to run a campaign from a hospital bed, Glenn resigned from the race. Two months later, he left the hospital. He went on sick leave from the Marine Corps in order to make a full recovery. He was promoted to the rank of colonel in October 1964 and retired from the Marine Corps in January 1965.

For the next several years, Glenn worked as an executive with Royal Crown International, a large soft drink company that makes RC Cola. He also made public appearances for NASA and the Boy Scouts. When Robert

"Bobby" Kennedy (John Kennedy's brother) decided to run for president, Glenn campaigned for him. ". . . as I saw Bobby feed off the crowds that supported him and listen to those who wanted to condemn him, it whetted my appetite for politics again," he said.[3]

In 1970, Ohio Senator Stephen M. Young said he would retire from the Senate. Glenn announced he would run for Young's seat. Glenn's campaign was badly organized and did not have much money. He lost, but he learned from the defeat. Glenn remained with Royal Crown until he won a seat in the Senate in November 1974. This time, his victory was big. He carried all eighty-eight counties in Ohio.[4] He was reelected in 1980 with the largest margin in Ohio history.

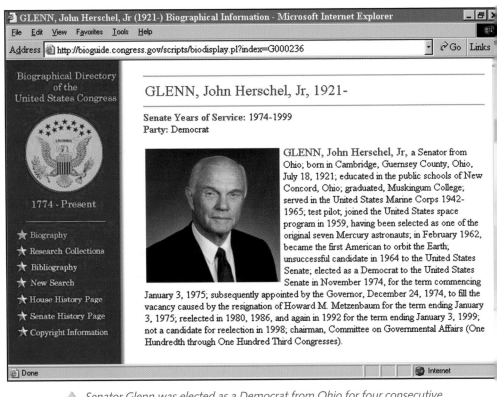

GLENN, John Herschel, Jr (1921-) Biographical Information - Microsoft Internet Explorer

File   Edit   View   Favorites   Tools   Help

Address 🖉 http://bioguide.congress.gov/scripts/biodisplay.pl?index=G000236   🔻 𝒞 Go Links

Biographical Directory
of the
United States Congress

1774 - Present

⭐ Biography
⭐ Research Collections
⭐ Bibliography
⭐ New Search
⭐ House History Page
⭐ Senate History Page
⭐ Copyright Information

GLENN, John Herschel, Jr, 1921-

Senate Years of Service: 1974-1999
Party: Democrat

GLENN, John Herschel, Jr, a Senator from Ohio; born in Cambridge, Guernsey County, Ohio, July 18, 1921; educated in the public schools of New Concord, Ohio; graduated, Muskingum College; served in the United States Marine Corps 1942-1965; test pilot; joined the United States space program in 1959, having been selected as one of the original seven Mercury astronauts; in February 1962, became the first American to orbit the Earth; unsuccessful candidate in 1964 to the United States Senate; elected as a Democrat to the United States Senate in November 1974, for the term commencing January 3, 1975; subsequently appointed by the Governor, December 24, 1974, to fill the vacancy caused by the resignation of Howard M. Metzenbaum for the term ending January 3, 1975; reelected in 1980, 1986, and again in 1992 for the term ending January 3, 1999; not a candidate for reelection in 1998; chairman, Committee on Governmental Affairs (One Hundredth through One Hundred Third Congresses).

🖉 Done   🌐 Internet

🔺 *Senator Glenn was elected as a Democrat from Ohio for four consecutive terms. He was the first senator from Ohio to accomplish this feat.*

▷ Glenn for President

In 1976, Jimmy Carter briefly considered Glenn for his running mate as vice president. After Carter was elected, Glenn decided his place to make a positive change was in the Senate. He said, "If I can have an impact on leaving the whole world a little better place some way through efforts in the Senate, I can't think of a better challenge. . . ."[5]

In 1983, Democratic Senator John Glenn's political values were opposite to Republican President Ronald Reagan's values. Glenn saw a chance to run for president. He announced he would run for the Democratic nomination. "My own life in some ways is what this country is all about," he said. ". . . My ambition is really for the country. You may think that's just talk, but it's what drove me in combat, it's what drove me in the space program, and it's what drives me to be president."[6]

Like his first Senate campaign, this race was also poorly organized. One *New York Times* reporter said, "Up to now, the Glenn campaign has been the greatest waste of a presidential candidate I've ever seen. They have an ideal candidate who has enormous popular appeal, but . . . there has been one of the worst organizational efforts I have ever seen."[7] Glenn dropped out of the race before the party's convention.

John Glenn's integrity came under attack in 1990. He was accused of using improper influence in a banking scandal. "I was very bitter at that time," Glenn said, "because it was so unfair. It was the low point, I guess, in my life because my ethics and my morality and . . . what I thought was right and wrong, were being challenged." The investigation's final report said Glenn had used "bad judgment" in arranging a luncheon between two parties but said Glenn had done "nothing wrong."[8]

▲ *Senator John Glenn speaks at a news conference on Capitol Hill in September 1998.*

▶ Accomplishments of Senator John Glenn

In 1992, Glenn made history again. He became the first senator from Ohio to be reelected to a fourth term in a row.

While in the Senate, Glenn became a member of both the Governmental Affairs Committee and of the Senate Armed Services Committee. He also served on the Select Committee on Intelligence and the Special Committee on Aging.

Glenn also challenged the bigotry that he felt existed there. The Senate had excluded itself from civil rights legislation. The employment requirements for a Senate job seemed to be, "no blacks," "white only," and "no secretaries who wear pantsuits." Glenn demanded an end to this discrimination.[9]

The senator was a strong supporter of federal funds for education. He supported the Equal Rights Amendment, and he was pro-choice on abortion. He had been in two wars and had seen the destruction of war. During his twenty-four years in the Senate, he tried to prevent the spread of nuclear weapons. He helped write the Nuclear Non-Proliferation Act of 1978. This act made it difficult for countries that did not have nuclear weapons to get them. In 1991, the Senate passed the Gulf War Resolution. Glenn opposed the resolution, feeling that the Gulf War was an excuse for the United States to gain more influence in the Middle East. After the war, Glenn sponsored laws to help the veterans and their families.

Glenn retired from the Senate at the age of seventy-five, when his fourth term expired in January 1999. He made his retirement announcement on February 20, 1997—the same day on which he had made his historic flight thirty-five years earlier. However, John Glenn was not retiring from public life. He had other plans.

RETURN TO SPACE

On John Glenn's first spaceflight, he brought back valuable information about the human body. He knew that astronauts faced physical changes in space. Astronauts have experienced bone loss and weakened muscles. Without gravity to put a load on the muscles and bones, they can dissolve away. For example, astronaut Dave Wolf flew two shuttle missions and spent more than 143 days in space. He lost 12 to 13 percent of bone mineral in his pelvis due to lack of gravity.[1] If Glenn could go into space again, scientists could study the effects of microgravity on his older body. The absence of gravity has a strange effect on the body. For instance, the immune system fights off diseases. In space, the immune system gets a little weaker. Scientists are not sure why. After studying Glenn, scientists might then find treatments for these issues facing the elderly on Earth.

Since Glenn's 1962 flight, astronauts have gone to the moon and worked aboard space stations. Still, space travel is dangerous. In January 1986, the Space Shuttle *Challenger* exploded killing all seven astronauts. Glenn did not think about what could go wrong. Instead, he thought about having a chance to serve his country again. "I was probably more nervous back in those days because we did not know much about space flight," said Glenn. "We were sort of feeling our way and finding out what would happen to the human body in space. . . ."[2]

Glenn spent two years try to persuade NASA to send him back into space. In January 1998, NASA announced that Glenn would be a member of the crew of the Space Shuttle *Discovery*, scheduled for launch later in the year. He was nearly twice the age of the average astronaut. At seventy-seven, he was the oldest person to fly in space.

Glenn's trip was not greeted warmly by everyone. Some said it was a publicity stunt. Others said it was a political "junket" (a trip without a serious agenda). Most people were enthusiastic. They saw Glenn's return to space as another act of courage. One journalist, writing in *Time* magazine, said not to listen to the people who call the mission useless. "The public does not require a usefulness beyond its own admiring pleasure. As for the

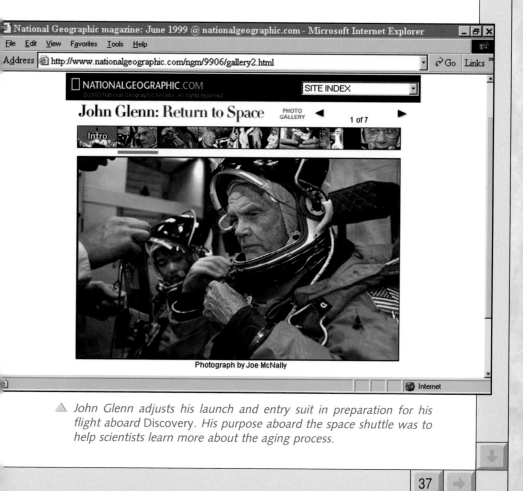

National Geographic magazine: June 1999 @ nationalgeographic.com - Microsoft Internet Explorer

File   Edit   View   Favorites   Tools   Help

Address http://www.nationalgeographic.com/ngm/9906/gallery2.html   Go   Links

NATIONALGEOGRAPHIC.COM   SITE INDEX

© 2003 National Geographic Society. All rights reserved

John Glenn: Return to Space   PHOTO GALLERY   ◀   1 of 7   ▶

Intro

Photograph by Joe McNally

Internet

△ *John Glenn adjusts his launch and entry suit in preparation for his flight aboard* Discovery. *His purpose aboard the space shuttle was to help scientists learn more about the aging process.*

practicalities of the space program, it was never so useful as when it reminded the country of heroic capabilities."[3]

Medical Research

Doctors took blood samples, measured Glenn's bones, and X-rayed his body. They would repeat these tests after his flight to see if his body had changed while in space. "One of the purposes of this flight," said Glenn, "is to see whether there is as much change in the body of older persons as there is in the younger people who are the rest of the crew up here now."[4]

Glenn was involved in two age-related experiments. He was both a researcher and a subject. One experiment studied the way certain proteins are processed during microgravity. "The vast majority of people seemed generally excited and intrigued by the possibility of a beginning to find answers about the aging process," said Glenn.[5] Scientists also hoped to learn about sleep patterns. They compared the biological clock that governs alertness and sleep between Glenn and the others in the crew. At one time, Glenn had twenty-one electrodes connected to his body to measure his sleep responses.[6] Glenn said,

I've had a lot of satisfaction out of my whole life of doing something . . . that I felt benefited other people. And now, at this point, going back up again or having the opportunity to benefit a lot of other people, I get a great deal of satisfaction out of that.[7] . . . I hope that by comparing what happens to me at my age in space with what happens to younger astronauts and with older people right here on Earth, maybe we can not only increase the ability of younger people to go on longer space flights, but also perhaps we can help eradicate many of the frailties of aging—things like balance and muscle system changes, osteoporosis and sleep disorders.[8]

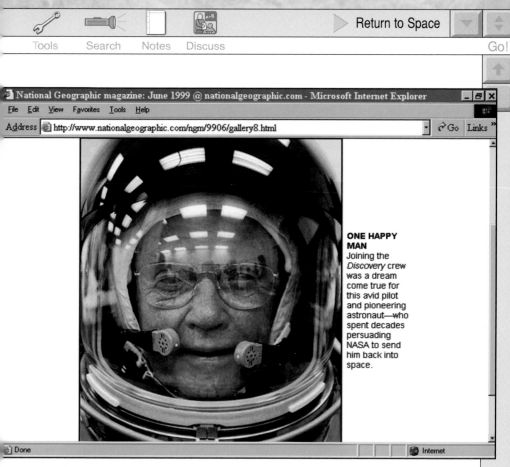

National Geographic magazine: June 1999 @ nationalgeographic.com - Microsoft Internet Explorer

File   Edit   View   Favorites   Tools   Help

Address   http://www.nationalgeographic.com/ngm/9906/gallery8.html   Go   Links

ONE HAPPY MAN
Joining the *Discovery* crew was a dream come true for this avid pilot and pioneering astronaut—who spent decades persuading NASA to send him back into space.

Done   Internet

▲ *At the age of seventy-seven, John Herschel Glenn, Jr., became the world's oldest astronaut.*

On Thursday, October 29, 1998, the crew climbed aboard the Shuttle *Discovery*. They strapped in and got ready for the launch. The vehicle shook and shuddered as its engines combined to produce more than 37 million horsepower of thrust.[9] "The vehicle was moving at 100 miles-per-hour by the time it cleared the tower," said Glenn.[10]

▷ An American Hero

Glenn and the *Discovery* crew returned to Earth on November 7. On Glenn's first spaceflight, he saw the sun rise and set three times from orbit. This flight was much

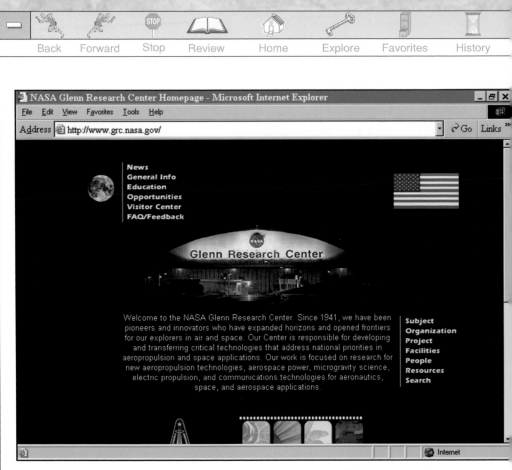

The NASA Lewis Research Center was renamed the NASA John H. Glenn Research Center at Lewis Field on March 1, 1999.

longer. On the *Discovery* flight, he flew 134 orbits and traveled 3.6 million miles. The flight proved that an older person could successfully take on difficult physical and mental challenges. Later, the test results suggested that there is no reason that older astronauts cannot continue going into space as active mission participants and research subjects.[11] The test results are also providing new information into how drugs produced in microgravity can fight cancerous tumors or help lessen the damage of bone cancer.[12] Later that month, Glenn and his wife, Annie, enjoyed their second ticker-tape parade in New York City.

▲ John Glenn's bravery and dedication to his country has earned him the reputation of a true American hero.

To honor Glenn, NASA renamed the Lewis Research Center, at Lewis Field in Glenn's home state of Ohio, the NASA John H. Glenn Research Center. NASA also awarded Glenn the Distinguished Service Medal and the Congressional Space Medal of Honor. Ohio State University opened the John Glenn Institute, where students can study politics.

A highway leading into Concord, Ohio, is named for him, as is the high school he attended in New Concord. Senator Glenn received the National Air and Space Museum Trophy for Lifetime Achievement, one of the Smithsonian Institution's highest awards. He also received the prestigious American Institute of Public Service's Jefferson Award in 2000 for his service as an elected official.

John Glenn had a long career dedicated to public service. He served his country as a combat pilot, war hero, test pilot, astronaut, and United States Senator. He was a successful soldier, businessman, politician, family man, and astronaut. John Glenn is a true American hero.

Chapter Notes

Chapter 1. "Godspeed, John Glenn"

1. *Mercury/Friendship 7* and Space Shuttle Discovery as of STS-95 Comparison <http://spaceflight.nasa.gov/shuttle/archives/sts-95/crew/mershut.html> (January 10, 2003).

2. John Glenn, Jr., "If You're Shook Up You Shouldn't Be There," *Life*, March 9, 1962, p. 25.

3. M. Scott Carpenter, John H. Glenn, Jr., and L. Gordon Cooper, et. al., *We Seven* (New York: Simon and Schuster, 1962), p. 383.

4. *John Glenn: A True American Hero.* Woodlands, Calif.: Westlake Entertainment Group, 1998, video recording.

5. Ibid.

6. Lloyd S. Swenson, Jr., James M. Grimwood, and Charles C. Alexander, "An American in Orbit," *This New Ocean: A History of Project Mercury,* 1989, <http://www.hq.nasa.gov/office/pao/History/SP-4201/ch13-4.htm#source40> (January 10, 2003).

7. Paul Mandel, "First Off it was Quite a Day," *Life*, March 2, 1962, p. 35.

8. Ibid., p. 35.

9. "John Glenn: 'I Want To Soak Up Every Bit of Experience I Can on This,'" *John Glenn: An American Hero*, 1998, <http://www.pbs.org/kcet/johnglenn/program/article/index.htm> (January 10, 2003).

Chapter 2. Growing Up

1. John Glenn with Nick Taylor, *John Glenn: A Memoir* (New York: Bantam Books, 1999), p. 10.

2. Ibid., p. 12.

3. Ibid., p. 11.

4. "John Glenn: 'I Want To Soak Up Every Bit of Experience I Can on This'" *John Glenn: An American Hero*, 1998, <http://www.pbs.org/kcet/johnglenn/program/article/index.htm> (January 10, 2003).

5. Ibid.

6. NASA, "Biographical Data," *John Glenn, Jr.,* January 1999, <http://www.jsc.nasa.gov/Bios/htmlbios/glenn-j.html> (January 10, 2003).

7. Glenn, p. 157.

8. Ibid., p. 158.

9. Blaine Baggett, "Transcript," *John Glenn: An American Hero*, 1998, <http://www.pbs.org/kcet/johnglenn/edresources/transcript/index.htm> (January 10, 2003).

Chapter 3. Project *Mercury*

1. Loyd S. Swenson, Jr., James M. Grimwood, and Charles C. Alexander, "Sputniks and Soul-Searching," *This New Ocean: A History of Project Mercury,* 1989, <http://www.hq.nasa.gov/office/pao/History/SP-4201/ch1-6.htm> (January 10, 2003).

2. Judy A. Rumerman, ed., "Mercury Missions," *Human Space Flight: A Record of Achievement, 1961–1998,* August 1998, <http://history.nasa.gov/40thann/humanspf.htm#mercury> (January 10, 2003).

3. Tom Wolfe, *The Right Stuff* (New York: Farrar-Straus-Giroux, 1979), p. 133.

4. Ibid., pp. 173–174.

5. "The Right Stuff," *John Glenn An American Hero,* 1998, <http://www.pbs.org/kcet/johnglenn/rightstuff/links/index.htm> (January 10, 2003).

Chapter 4. *Friendship 7*

1. Robert Godwin, ed., *Friendship 7: The First Flight of John Glenn, The NASA Mission Reports* (Ontario, Canada: Apogee Books, 1999), p. 119.

2. M. Scott Carpenter, John H. Glenn, Jr., and L. Gordon Cooper, *We Seven* (New York: Simon and Schuster, 1962), p. 382.

3. Steve Siceloff, "Last of Mercury 7 mark historic flight into orbit," *Space: Floridatoday.com,* February 25, 2002, <http://www.floridatoday.com/news/space/stories/2002a/022502mercury.htm> (January 10, 2003).

4. Ibid.

5. Carpenter, et. al., p. 385.

6. Godwin, p. 118.

7. Ibid., p. 120.

8. Paul Mandel, "First Off it was Quite a Day," *Life*, March 2, 1962, p. 39.

9. Loyd S. Swenson, Jr., James M. Grimwood, and Charles C. Alexander, "An American in Orbit," *This New Ocean: A History of Project Mercury,* 1989, <http://www.hq.nasa.gov/office/pao/History/SP-4201/ch13-4.htm#source39> (January 10, 2003).

10. Mandel, p. 35.

11. Godwin, pp. 126, 200.

12. Ibid., p. 128.

13. Ibid. pp. 128–129.

14. *John Glenn: A True American Hero.* Woodlands, Calif.: Westlake Entertainment Group, 1998, video recording.

15. Godwin, p. 132.

16. John Glenn, "Space is the Frontier of My Profession," "A Giant Leap for Mankind," n.d., <http://www.life.com/Life/space/giantleap/sec3/glenn1.html> (January 10, 2003).

17. "John Glenn: 'I Want To Soak Up Every Bit of Experience I Can on This,'" 1998, <http://www.pbs.org/kcet/johnglenn/program/article/index.htm> (January 10, 2003).

Chapter 5. Public Service

1. Richard F. Fenno, Jr., *The Presidential Odyssey of John Glenn* (Washington, D.C.: Congressional Quarterly Press, 1990), p. 6.

2. John Glenn with Nick Taylor, *John Glenn: A Memoir* (New York: Bantam Books, 1999), p. 304.

3. Ibid., p. 322.

4. Ibid., p. 331.

5. Peter N. Carroll, *Famous in America—The Passion to Succeed* (New York: E. P. Dutton, 1985), p. 255.

6. Ibid., p. 265.

7. Phil Gailey, "Glenn Field Drive Launched in Iowa," *New York Times,* November 7, 1983, p. A–19.

8. Blaine Baggett, "Transcript," *John Glenn: An American Hero,* 1998, <http://www.pbs.org/kcet/johnglenn/edresources/transcript/index.htm> (January 10, 2003).

9. Carroll, p. 257.

Chapter 6. Return to Space

1. *Inside the Space Station,* Discovery Channel Video, Discovery Channel Films, LLC., 2000.

2. "STS-95 Educational Downlink," n.d., <http://spaceflight .nasa.gov/shuttle/archives/sts-95/transcripts/fd3edutranscript .html> (January 10, 2003).

3. Essay by Roger Rosenblatt, "A Realm Where Age Doesn't Count," 1998, <http://www.digitaljournalist.org/issue9810/ glenn01.htm> (January 10, 2003).

4. "STS-95 Educational Downlink."

5. John Glenn with Nick Taylor, *John Glenn: A Memoir* (New York: Bantam Books, 1999), p. 369.

6. Carla Garnett, "'Next Flight, Please,'" *National Institutes of Health,* 1999, <http://www.nih.gov/news/NIH-Record/ 01_26_99/story01.htm> (January 10, 2003).

7. Blaine Baggett, "Transcript," *John Glenn: An American Hero,* 1998, <http://www.pbs.org/kcet/johnglenn/edresources/ transcript/index.htm> (January 10, 2003).

8. Garnett, "'Next Flight, Please.'"

9. NASA Facts FS-2000-05-104 MSFC.

10. Glenn, p. 393.

11. Ibid., Epilogue, p. 407.

12. Leonard David, "John Glenn's Shuttle Flight Seen As Boon to Biomedical Research," *Science/Astronomy,* 2002, <http://www.space.com/scienceastronomy/planetearth/space_heal th_000128.html> (January 10, 2003).

Books

Bond, Peter. *Guide to Space.* New York: Dorling Kindersley, Inc., 1999.

Bredeson, Carmen. *John Glenn Returns to Orbit, Life on the Space Shuttle.* Berkeley Heights, N.J.: Enslow Publishers, 2000.

Burgan, Michael. *John Glenn: Young Astronaut.* New York: Aladdin Paperbacks, 2000.

Cole, Michael D. *Friendship 7: First American in Orbit.* Springfield, N.J.: Enslow Publishers, 1995.

Farndon, John. *The Giant Book of Space.* Brookfield, Conn.: Copper Beach Books, 2000.

Kramer, Barbara. *John Glenn: A Space Biography.* Berkeley Heights, N.J.: Enslow Publishers, 1998.

Lammers, Laura, ed. *A Hero Born: A Tribute to John Glenn.* Knoxville, Tenn.: A Poet Born Press, 1999.

Stott, Carole. *Space Exploration.* New York: Alfred A. Knopf, 1997.

Streissguth, Tom. *John Glenn.* Minneapolis, Minn.: Lerner Publications, 1999.

Vogt, Gregory. *John Glenn's Return to Space.* Brookfield, Conn.: Millbrook Press, 2000.

Video

John Glenn: A True American Hero. Woodlands, Calif.: Westlake Entertainment Group, 1998, video recording.

0001200694337
J B GLENN
Holden, Henry M.
Trailblazing astronaut John
6/01/04